Melissa Emily Fuentes was born on January 10, 2008 as the youngest of three sisters in Los Angeles, CA, with a fiery passion for music. She is a young new author who can always be found with her heart, her Siberian Husky, who is the most precious, loving, and gentle, "girl's best friend," along with her other best friend, Manny. Every free moment she has is spent on reading, writing and listening to her music. She wears her heart on her sleeve and pours it out in her writing. *The Honey Bee Rivals the Spring*, compilation of poems that takes you, the reader, on a journey with her that you soon will find yourselves starting to expand your minds and explore your innermost thoughts and feelings. You will find yourselves feeling supported and empowered as you begin to truly relate to the painted pictures of self-discovery and understanding of your own most inner thoughts. As you read on, you will begin to start accepting your past heart-breaks, shortcomings, disappointments, betrayals, and hurts you have experienced. You will realize you are not alone, and when you're at your lowest points is when you can learn how to unconditionally love yourself and find your greatest strength.

Melissa's dream is to share her love of words and the magic words create when they are carefully placed together in a way that they come alive. So alive that they shine light for others when traveling down their dark roads, so that they can always be sure the rainbow will reveal itself when the storm is over.

My mom, dad, my best friend Manny,
and my baby husky Sativa.

Melissa Fuentes

THE HONEYBEE RIVALS THE SPRING

AUSTIN MACAULEY PUBLISHERS™

LONDON • CAMBRIDGE • NEW YORK • SHARJAH

Ordering Information
Quantity sales: Special discounts are available on quantity purchases by corporations, associations, and others. For details, contact the publisher at the address below.

Publisher's Cataloging-in-Publication data
Fuentes, Melissa
The Honeybee Rivals the Spring

ISBN 9781685629120 (Paperback)
ISBN 9781685629137 (Hardback)
ISBN 9781685629144 (ePub e-book)

www.austinmacauley.com/us

First Published 2024
Austin Macauley Publishers LLC
40 Wall Street, 33rd Floor, Suite 3302
New York, NY 10005
USA

mail-usa@austinmacauley.com
+1 (646) 5125767

I would like to acknowledge my mom because she is the driving force behind me, always encouraging and supporting me. I get my love of literature from her. My dad was the first person to acknowledge my passion for writing and was the one who encouraged me to submit my very first manuscript. Manny, is the best friend I could ever hope for. He has been such an intricate part of my life, always by my side through all the challenges in my life and my sisters Isabel and Elaina may not always see eye to eye with me. However, at the end of the day we will always put everything aside and be there for each other. My baby husky Sativa is my child, and my life without her would be dull, colorless and empty. She brings me so much joy and love!

My papa Richard Ernest Alcala and my grandma Josephina Barbosa Alcala, may they rest in peace. They helped care for me and my sisters and were a vital part of my life. They always helped keep me grounded and made sure I felt loved. They always made sure my stomach was full!

I Am Not a Messenger Man

Ever since images have created within my mind I have
always been in the middle of the line
A tightrope that I have never wanted, one sway to the right
I'm gone, to the left I'm gone
But with words multiplying on top of hearts and thoughts, I
thought I could pick and be happy but I couldn't
Every word would hurt me
Every word I spoke created crevices in the heart of me
I was taught so much
but something that has affected my every wave, was how I
should calm the storm
but how could I?
The storm dances with my family
an agony, a cycle they never seemed to fully go through
How could my words alone finish the storm, I have tried
But the only thing I accomplished was making a fury of hail
fall upon me:
"Am I right?"
"Am I lying?"
"Tell me I am wrong?"
"What did you hear?"
were questions, well more like threats, I have answered with
hesitance
Bubbles floated to the bottom every time
How could I know what to do
What should I do

They both want to hear different things but with the fear
swelling my thoughts how could I think
One moment I am loved and the storm is out of eyes reach
The next I am nothing more than a speck in the wind that
gets trapped in people eyes
a small insignificance
an annoyance
how could I?

What We Create

Neglectful mother
Hurtful father
The fire is always changing faster than weather
The black and white clouds mix above our heads, swaying
with the wind
It all comes rumbling in with the soft comfort that would
eventually kill us
Time and time again
Filling the knot of loose ends
Creating a form of art from the needles of our hatred
The hatred created
The hatred created with every part and portion of our
worthless souls.

Generational Beauty

Should I become my ice-walled mom
or my forest-fire dad
The only thing I ever accomplished was making them more mad
through my sister's eyes I see my father
through my sister's eyes I see my mother
through my eyes
I see the hatred of generations mixing inside my pupils,
unsolicited memories wrapped around the basement of my mind
I feel the tingles after the fire
and the shame after the creaking
But I still sleep on the bed my parents made me
Is it hereditary or taught?
A question that has occurred to me in the memories of my heart
for I too am a forest fire.

Diamonds

Emotions fueled by thoughts
Thoughts of the throat cutting screams
And the even more glass-shattering tears
A diamond crafted by my family's hand
It glimmers with sparkles in the light
Perhaps others would call it strong
To withstand all the heat
But the fire that has reached
Reached the most detrimental parts of me.

Dreams

A trance from an illuminated carrier on the back of the ground
My vision dances with the sky
trickles of lightning dust clogged in my lunges
My tongue feels like saw dust with traces of war rocks
Dying on a stage where billions of eyes look in wonder at a crime scene
With their eyes sparkling, they say, "I can take that."
Once too many times have the barrier from the surface towards the heart have been severed
I may not be brilliant
But I'll follow the sun till even my own skin melts, with my eyeballs submerging in my veins
There is a light I scream in my darkened dream
An image of thoughts piling towards mars with diamonds surrounded
I stand alone,
in a universe with no place to call home.

Hope

For the pullings and pushings I stand tall
Below me is misty rocks that I hope I'll never see again
A pitch looming darkness shines brightly below me
I take breaths
As I made it to the edge you took my hand
you twirled me with the wind for what felt like a second
Then you pushed
I walked to the edge just for you to push me off
And as I fell to my death, I saw you standing there
With your pitch perfect smile that turned into a murderous
glare
I walked on this tightrope just for you
Only for you to push me off once I finally get to you
All the venom you've put inside of me
I've taken gladly
And when you calm down
I'll wait for when you say you're sorry as you let my hand
go
Cause I know that your words mean nothing in the end
cause no matter what you say my body is
still at the bottom of the cliff
Maggots swarm around my remains and worms infest in my
brain
And no words can make them go away
But I'll still visit my own grave, getting your favorite
flowers in hopes you'll see me through
Hoping it'll revive whatever love you have for me left
If there is any at all.

Believe

I have anchored my mind on places which have tainted me
My heart beats to sirens of a never-ending sleep
They ring ring ring
More than my father's swears or my mother's glares
I have looked in the eyes of the very pain that has kept me
in this place
so why am I still writing on the same bruised wall
on the wall of my heart
A door that I created with lines and inks of a feather trailed
upon it
I have seen what people perceive as evil
And I have created evil within myself
People simply helped stacked the blocks of every thought
that has tormented me
every thought that has come from me
My mumbles made the stars twinkle
for moments I felt as if I was soaked in stardust
But from moments on make believe elephants I realize now
that that's exactly what it was
make believe
I was almost hoping for an end of my own mind
The very mind that has taught me so much
The mind that has grown with black mist around every
corner
But the thing that has ruined me the most
was when the pain became numb
A calm

quiet numb that has washed over every inch of my mind

Which has written upon daggers and scars which were drawn from my own hand

undoubtedly, caressing the slain beings from my veins, consequently on every page

On even my own name.

I Have to Think Fast

All the pain in my veins
that has fallen upon me
It's my chance and I have to think fast to put it all behind
me
I have built myself a womb that I can live inside and
I have crafted all my plans and synced it to my heart beat
I have created an ideology of which has forsaken me
Trying to write through my past has never really phased me
I understand I may not be the best in all my faces
but on the path of self-reflection and realization, I found
myself waiting for the trains end
With caution and mild preparation, I found a figure worth a
name
Attaining it was the strain
Colored blocks of my thoughts from my childhood face
An instance of ludicrously entraining in my veins.

Traces of Innocence

Confusion I have always known
I have never known the truth to my parents
Not in their purest
Not in their ugliest
I have never understood the way they loved
From harsh words and yelling
to soft murmurs and kisses
It was a never-ending cycle of the same recurrence
just a different setting
I never *really* knew who was telling the truth
They both said the opposite things with the same amount of
hate
the same amount of vain
their words swarming with the lies of my heart
Fighting for ignorance and searching for traces
traces of importance
traces of remembrance
traces of nothingness.

Understanding Love

I never understood the concept of love, or even missing
someone
For we are animals, primal beings with attachments
So on my journey of sociopathy and narcissism
I carved a desire, a figment to reach
An idea I couldn't speak
I finally realized that love is not supposed to be dissected in
labs
And that no one I have seen has ever realized how it truly
feels to love, or be loved
But at the same time, we all have felt that sequence and that
gloating
And I honestly can't comprehend the fact that it took
missing someone to finally understand that
Because I realized that I am capable of love
perhaps not capable enough for someone to love me
but the minor detail that I can love, is enough for me
I have seen and been many things
I have felt every form of love
Every form of self-gratification and self-mutilation
And through every piece of me carved on the walls of my
mind that I have built, I loved
and loved.

Wishes

Tears trace my face as I pack and run away
The war in my home matched the war in my mind
I remember feeling free with a blank memory on the line
A feeling now foreign if it ever revives
A loophole of never-ending endings circulating my world
I thought I heard a whisper of hope only to find it was just
the wind
But still I have wishful thinking
as I trace the scars of the living
and run away, once again.

Forevermore

Everybody was dying the year I was born
I was born into a world of confusion and hurt
A world of fear and anguish
As my cries filled every corner of a singular hospital room
The whole world was crying too
And for moments I thought that they were crying with me
But with moments came endings
and emotions came leavings
And with finances came crashes
multiple cases of unjust and abuse
cases of brutality that lives on in humanity
sharp caresses and forgiving adolescents
will live on, forevermore.

Inevitably

Barren heads gleam towards the morning sun
I am too afraid to die, I tried once and I never
I was born starving for an ounce of a tree
an ominous feeling, that appears when I starve
Afraid for what is behind the curtain, Afraid to wake up
after a midnight rest
Wishes of closing my eyes forever
Wishes and promises made from thorns of porcupines
surrounding my bones
I no longer wish to feel the burning sun
or the freezing snow
But I want to feel the warmth the sun brings
and the relief the snow gives me
Drenching my body in thoughts passed down onto me
The pain is hereditary
The hunger was passed down from my mother's mother
and my father's father
And will continue, inevitably.

Chrysanthemums

Chrysanthemums were always my favorite flower
For they are vibrant and beautiful
My great grandmother loved them as well
gentle hands and a gentle soul
that's what I would describe her as
When we had no one, she housed us
The Christmas presents by the tree
the cards she gave to every parent
and the gifts to every kid
I was a child, not knowing how blessed I was for every
ounce of pennies she paid for every single being that barely
knew her
But I did
I knew her
Me and my sisters used to dress up in her much too large
for us nightgowns
And I loved curling up to her gentle lap
as we watched a cartoon that she got from the place west of
her home
She had gentle hands
gentle beautiful hands
The moments when we were gone, I barely said a word to
her, not understanding how fast someone could go
The doctor and his pity filled sigh
The doctor and his micro concern
He's done this many times
So we took her home
made sure she was comfortable
and then let her go
Chrysanthemums were always my favorite flower
till I felt the weight of it glow.

Permanent

The river that was thirty minutes away from my papa's
house evaporated
I honestly didn't even notice it until it was gone
I look upon from where I sat in the back of my mother's car
I felt like crying, and I didn't even know why
My papa who I used to live with would always laugh at
around ten pm
I would hear him from my room as he laughed
And I use to not think of it 'cause it was always there
till it wasn't
I realized how lively he made the house seem
How his laugh would fill up every corner of the house for
years
Until one day, it was gone
and I realized how it was there, so prominent in the air
I guess I thought it'd be permanent
like how I thought the river would be
I never noticed the river was there till it was gone
well of course I noticed it but I always thought it'd be
permanent.

Quiet

The velvet sky
turned fury red that day
I remember the feeling
From the waiting to the room
the fear of the unknown, of change
bad change
You were quiet, more quiet than the most peaceful nights
when you rested your eyes
This is the first time
I remember
This is the first time you were silent
The first time I saw you stare off into a white cold wall
it was quiet
As the clatter and loud hurried chatter from five feet away
rang loud in my ears
it was quiet
As I stared at you
it was quiet
I remember this being the first time I saw you so vulnerable
and I thought
These masked faced people don't know you
They don't know your fierce will and your gentle heart
They don't know how you would always take us around the
park
with laughter and full bellies for hours
And as we both stare
probably with similar timeless thoughts

or maybe with thoughts entirely different
we both knew, everything will change
And not the good change like getting that puppy you always
wanted
or passing your driver's test
no, this was entirely different
So as we both get lost in the sea of our thoughts
we all knew, it would all change
And for the first time in my life
it was quiet.

Directionless

My words fade out in the background of crowds from movie screens
Simply existing to lessen space
Simply there, in the background
feeling the air that surrounds me everywhere
For I am directionless, not knowing which way the wind comes from
Simply everywhere and simply no where
For my existence is nothing more than questions in the multitude of existence
Forever, never changing, forever
I know I am not pretty, not me or my words, my thoughts or my feelings
For I am unworthy, nothing more than
a leech that needs a bigger, a better vessel to consume of
For I am nothing but a grain of sand which belongs to a bigger entity
And which I am not, inevitably.

Question

The question occurred in a memory
A distant fog clouded my mind
As the grey question mark came to me
I wish I could say it was in vain
but I pondered on it
I wandered in my mind trying make sense of a question
without an answer
I wander I wander I wander
As I pass hazes of memory I am stopped
An invisible block that looks so much like me keeps me in
place
Searching for ways through
but to find there is none
So I open up a window
just to feel the cold air tingle my skin for a moment of
remanence
But even with the window I can't seem to find the answer
in my mind
I know it's here somewhere
Maybe somewhere north
But the block is keeping me from searching further than the
window's peak
And I cannot seem to see from the fog that is circulating me
Time passes and the memory of the question becomes a
dizzy haze
Now I'm stuck trying to find an answer to a question
a question unknown to me.

Sunday Mornings

My family once asked me,
"What happened to you?"
As I stopped being a kid and became a teen
No, they actually didn't say a thing
But my thoughts came up with phantoms of pain
and I do wonder, how'd I get this way
First grade was when it really first started
the constant checking of my waistline
The kids that would point and compare me to the school's
brick walls
I never starved – no
My love for food was a comfort I felt no one else knew
Instead I checked and checked and checked
When I was younger my arms were smaller
When I grew taller, so did the checking
I remember getting a haircut on a Sunday morning
I was embarrassed, ashamed, afraid of constant judging
So I was quiet and said nothing
And afterwards I wish I did
'cause after that I never said anything ever again.

Maybe

I never really had a clear answer as to why when people asked
Even I don't know, but I think it has something to do with trying to make sense of my pain, the pain that has no physical bruises or scars
But I felt most of all
Sometimes I think it was to punish myself, for who am I to cry when there's so much heartache in the world
Or maybe I did something wrong
Maybe it's just simply my brain that has wronged me, or perhaps I have wronged my brain
So even now if you ask me why, I wouldn't really have a clear answer
but maybe just maybe I'll understand why
if you ever do.

Eggshells

Observing everything
The backyard, the kitchen, the bathrooms you don't ever use
Just to find something
Find something wrong
Because I come from the wrong blood
Walking on eggshells for nothing
Walking on eggshells in every house I've ever laid my head
on
I never felt the warm embrace of a home
a warm, safe home
I've always had a reason to be alert
Sensing every energy to know if I can enter
But I never really had a choice, did I?

Senses

I know you are much older than I
but I deserve respect too
For I am still human no matter my age
We mess around just how you fight
But I can tell when you will burn me
And for days that go by I try with all my might
It's like a disconnection from the view
even my vision is new
A familiarity I've always known
I hear you laugh from the floor
I can sense the energy you bestow
even when you laugh, I know.

Everything No One Knows

I wonder if they knew what would they do
would they cradle me like a mother would her child
Or shame me like the people in my school
I need to get up and take a shower
Clean off layers and layers of dirt that no one knows about
but me
My hips they are weak
My insides feel the sand paper that has been glued inside of
me
My legs tremble as I stumble from gravity
I'll wash thoroughly
Trying to take off phantom dirt that is my skin
If only a zipper would appear
So I could come out of the very body I took my first breath
in
Or maybe even just peel, it squishes together and I breath
1, 2, 3
then I peel
Stretching my skin till it's enough for every whisper
unspoken
every whisper unheard.

Forget You

Playgrounds would glisten with the evening glare
We would laugh all day with our hands in the air
And I remember your smile as you took me there
But now you live in the front of my mind
a memory, a parasite I can never forget
I try to find and salvage some pieces of you
But as it is, you are no one to be found
For you reside in my heart and he resides in my sight
But as it is, a sparrow flies over my head, as I lay,
dreaming of you.

My Sisters

Every day I write the same tears
"I am tired"
But nonetheless I am still right here
wishing I could be more like my sisters
distant, cold, not fragile to the unfulfilled promises of love
But I am none of those
I try to, but it's useless
for I am weak to my father's tears
I want to scream, "You're losing me,"
But knowing me I can't
Hoping he'd do something despicable
Just so I can stop forgiving the very loving eyes that hate
me
But knowing me, I probably will
For I am weak and that is that
Like a lion killing its prey
I can try to survive, but so be my doom
For I can never change
And neither can he.

Sea Wind

I remember looking out the window from my childhood
home
I use to look at the sunset skies and think it was lava
as the red and orange created a perspective of love
Addicted to the fury of the sun as it sets for loon
I tried to believe the shade of red was yellow and lilac blue
Mistaking the abuse for love
And the love for manipulation
So as I write this from an abandoned cocooned nest
I trace my fingers of the salted moon
tasting the sting right after
And I feel the casting of the wind straight to the heart of the
sea
come
right back to me.

My Sister's Teachings

My sister taught me many things
like how to tie my shoes when we were small
And how to sit and argue properly
with her head raised tall
My sister taught me many things
like how to silent my tears that roll down my ruby red
swollen cheeks
as she snarls and bites at me
You broke all my fingers and bones
when all I ever wanted was a home
The fear of being alone
has made a bed in my head
from all your venom that you poured into me
You can ask for a leaf and I'll give you a tree
and still, it's never enough
As your words become burns that have flooded my home
And the scars that are invisible that have severed deeper
than the one's seen
Yet you still pour your poison into me
My sister taught me many things
but the one that still resonates within me
is the fact I can bring her a tree
and still, I'll never be enough
For the unlovable part is within me.

I Love You

If you can't stop using for me
at least stop using for you
I put my love on rivers
I put my love on oceans
hoping it'll rain all over you
But I know our time is due
For you have a way of showing me when our time is up
From the roughness of your walk
to the ugliness in your face it creates
it all crumbles with the rain
And with every spark of flame burning
I love you, I love you, I love you.

Innocent

No more feeling free while jumping on a trampoline
From playgrounds and play rooms
to the end with you
The torch scarred the inside of my thighs
as my innocent mind said bye
And I still remember the moments with you
as we laid down and I became a fool
And you probably never think of it
but every day I feel it
The way the innocent touches became tainted
The touches that were once playful morphed into a sticky
poison
The poison which has dirtied my insides
from my mind to my frame it all became
dirty
and by association I was made dirty
And even then, I could never actually blame you
For you are dirty too.

Borrowed Time

Walking upon bookshelves with a glimmer in our eyes
Time feels like an afterthought in this moment of life
Syncing towards an afterlife while losing borrowed time
Tying bolts of lightning with each zap heading straight
towards the sun of me
Running from a boulder built of violent machinery
Forever
With a shimmer in your eyes of fire dust
as I try to dust off the remains of our love from old
bookshelves filled with stories of us.

9 781685 629120